ISBN: 978-1-66782-811-4

QUILTED POEMS

An Ekphrastic Collaboration of Quilters and Poets

Editor: Kathleen P. Decker

Associate Editor: Terry Cox-Joseph

Curated by Kathleen P. Decker

Acknowledgments:

This book contains the work of a large number of people, and was produced by the combined efforts of the Poetry Society of Virginia, Colonial Piecemakers Quilt Guild, and the Art Quilt Tribe of Studio Art Quilters Associates. The editors would like to thank all who participated in the creation of this book.

These works appeared as a Special Exhibit at the Mancuso Mid-Atlantic Quilt Show, February 24-27, 2022 in Hampton, Virginia, where each quilt was displayed with one or more of the poems. Thanks to David Mancuso and his show staff for welcoming our exhibit!

Special thanks to Ms. Terry Cox-Joseph, current President of the Poetry Society of Virginia, for her work as Associate Editor of this collection. Finally, we are deeply grateful to Harry Morrow, who professionally photographed most of the quilts for this book. ww.HarryMorrowPhotography.com

Foreword:

As the president of the Poetry Society of Virginia, I am thrilled to introduce *An Ekphrastic Collaboration of Quilters and Poets.* I have participated in ekphrastic events many times, both as an artist and writer, but this is the first time I have participated in an event that involved quilts. Because of the limits of fabric, scissors, machine-and hand-stitching, quilt-making presents challenges and opportunities not otherwise present in typical 2D or sculptural work. I offer a heartfelt, "Bravo!" to all.

One of the main challenges I perceived was how to approach and respond to an abstract concept, as is the wont of so many poets, in the form of a quilt? The response to those challenges is enlightening. For example, Obelia Akanke, in her poem, "Have you ever?" asks, "Have you ever tried to hold light?" Her poem concludes with: "Maybe, just maybe, you'll be close enough to shine together," to which quilter Emma Allen responds with a silhouette of a man and a woman reaching toward one another from trapezes. Between rainbow colors, a vertical strip of light runs the length of the quilt and highlights a space between the acrobats' hands—an apt visual that lends a sense of materiality to abstraction.

In "Cutting New Fabric," Denise Wilcox begins, "I lost myself/ In the meadow." Annabel Ebersole writes in her artist statement, "…Some flower stems are painted using the edge of a hotel door key. Other flowers are stitched, such as the French knots for the Queen Anne's Lace. The path meanders gently around the torn edges of the linen allowing the viewer to dream and plan." What we see is nothing like a standard quilt, but an impressionistic, hand-rendered, 3D painting of sorts, that clearly indicates a field of flowers with tiny, white, loose threads winding around horizontal sections of wildflowers. Immerse yourself in this 3D world, both literal and imaginary, and enjoy.

—Terry Cox-Joseph, President, Poetry Society of Virginia, author of **Between Then and Now** and other works.

Preface:

This book was created as an ekphrastic collaboration of poets of the Poetry Society of Virginia, and quilters from Virginia. Ekphrastic is Greek for to 'describe or explain.' The quilts in this book visually describe poems written to inspire quilters. Some quilters used concrete depictions of the poem, such Jeanne Sanders depicting a house with roses for Sandy Robinette's poem *Amen Roses*. Others utilized abstract symbols, such as Corrine Vance, who used "flying geese" quilt blocks to depict flying birds for Sally Zakariya's poem "Murmuration of Starlings." It was a joy to incorporate such diverse and imaginative works into the finished book.

—Dr. Kathleen P. Decker, Editor, author of **Nature, Love & the Psychiatrist** and other works

Table of Contents:

Curator's Note:

Some poems inspired multiple quilters to make quilts. For visual purposes in this book, some quilts were placed facing other poems. The Artist's Statements on pages 116-119 reflect the quilters' inspiration and plan.

Legends of quilts include the following desingations:
In the legends, **Quilt**: refers to the individual who designed, pieced, and quilted it. If it was quilted by another person (layers stitched together) that person is identified in the legend. Both are listed in the Quilters Index.

QUILTS AND QUILTERS

A Gift That Keeps on Giving

by Clay Harrison

Some of life's fondest memories

    involve quilts someone made,

Someone special who sewed each stitch

    with a love that never fades.

In childhood days, we were poor

    and Winters were quite cold

In low-rent housing where a quilt

    was a treasure to behold.

Mom often burned the "midnight oil"

    quilting through the years

After working dawn to dusk

    when we were in arrears.

Outgrown clothes turned into patches,

    each one a memory,

Sacred pages from life's album

    that grew our family tree.

Every grandchild got a special quilt

    crafted by Grandma's hands,

Hands that once rocked my cradle,

    praying hands that understand.

There's no gift quite as precious

    that's found in any store.

It's a gift that keeps on giving…

    need I say anymore?

Cutting New Fabric

by Denise Wilcox

I lost myself
In the meadow.
Tall grasses hid my feet.
"If I stand here
Long enough
Perhaps
I'll root and grow
Into something else.

"You appear downcast."

My glance did cast down
To where my stability
Once was.
A thousand blue eyes
Met mine.
Chicory.
Sturdy stems,
Rough-edged leaves,
Powder blue wisdom.

"Have you considered
Ripping out those seams?
The ones that bind
And suffocate you?"

"Too many stitches.
Too many tiny tight stitches.
It would ruin my fabric.

"Queen Anne,
What say you?"

Pale green, delicate stems
Tilted their lacey white blooms
Straight to my heart.

"I say, start ripping.
Your material will
Persevere."

You don't know me.

"You don't know you.
Chicory and I have
Weathered drought
And torrent, too.
If we can bloom
In profusion,
You can."

Perhaps I can start
In one corner.
Begin patching
Pieces together.
Pure white.
Dusty blue.
Lush green.

"Pick up your feet.
Cut that new fabric.
Use old scraps
Worth saving.
Create your own design."

My fingers threaded
Gently over the meadow
Wildflowers.
I set my feet toward home.
Ready to begin.

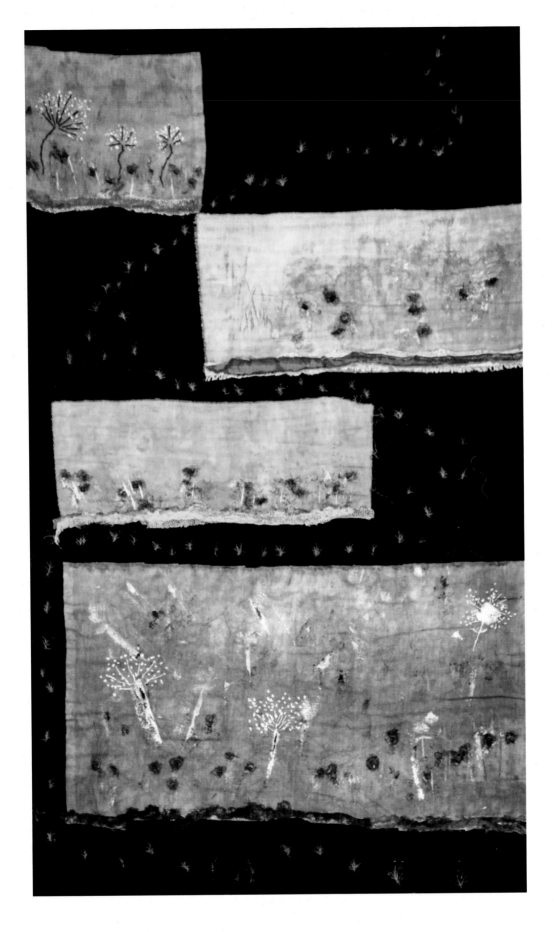

Quilt: Annabel Ebersole **Photo**: Harry Morrow

Quilting

by Marjorie Gowdy

Pretty sure I turned out the worst,
the watcher,
the plain one who gathers stories under the quilt
and shuffles a deck as each drifts into dreams.
Fastening fables embroidering a seam of memory on the snowy trip home.

Cousins bundle under Granny's two layers of hand-stitching
in an old farmhouse the airport took on rolling land in the Valley
where Grandad had started poor, so poor, and angry, so angry, near Sangersville,
and ended a happy man with a crock of butter, slaughtered hogs,
cherry jam, and us.

He was laughing and dancing on top of the coffin,
my brother swore. Both passed in '81, Grandad in winter and Billy in fall,
bound by the gentle undercurrent disguised
by rapids of sorrow
bred in generations never met.

Granny lived forever. I whispered to her:
Grandad plays with your long dark locks. You unpin them only for him.
On bright morns as the hay dried and bees teased the honeysuckle,
Granny weeds vegetables.
She plants hollyhocks among tomatoes.

She quilts on rainy days.
I hide in the sleeping porch
arrange sepia pictures of my uncles in the war
into piles of Pacific and Atlantic
into piles of old girlfriends.

Granny feeds the hogs with a loud 'souie' and names them, names gone by
butchering in November.
She grabs a chicken makes hot lunch on Sundays.
She feeds everyone first,
sips chicory coffee from a china saucer as we eat.

Quilt: Joan Johnson **Photo**: Harry Morrow

Seasons of the Heart

by Clay Harrison

Every quilt is someone's treasure,
       every pattern unique.
They can be so awe-inspiring
       that we can hardly speak.
Like pieces of a jigsaw puzzle,
       every square has its place
To form the patterns of our lives
       with dignity and grace.

Loving hands arrange the squares
       and form a work of art
That on the coldest Winter night
       warms the body and the heart.
Once upon a quilting party,
       Grandma's friends came by
And they made some precious memories
       that make us laugh and cry.

Every pattern tells a story,
       each in its own way.
What better gift to give a bride
       to bless her wedding day?
There's are many seasons of the heart
       that warm us like a smile,
And quilts are those special gifts
       that are always in style!

Quilt: Joan Johnson   **Photo**: Harry Morrow

The Love of Counterpane

by Beth Simpson Huddleston

The timeless stitches,
each made with delicate care,
created patterns in the white
cotton ---
While meticulous colors
produced secure, but artistic
designs.
And we studied them
for hours ---
laughing over this shirt,
remembering that dress,
recalling those shorts ---
All made with the same
love and skill
as the beautiful
cover
on the bed.
It was something she did ---
and we wouldn't know
until we were older
not a skill,
but truly an art.
Just as her many other
ways of loving:
the intricate, tatted lace,
the elegant dance dress,
the tingling Kool-Aid spiked with 7-Up,
the peaches and Milky Ways frozen
in the freezer,

the egg custard, bread, sauerkraut,
and pigs' feet,
the two little rooster plates
hidden in the towel drawer
for two special boys,
the sash tied perfectly,
a haven where no make-believe
game was too silly ---
Each act as full of
thought and caring
as the stitches
in the bedcover.
An act of creating
a secure place to close
one's eyes
at the end
of a weary day:
the love of counterpane,
the love of a grandmother

My Spanish Veil

by Marorie Gowdy

My grandmother called it tatting, tightly woven cotton strands

curled, warped,

pinned neatly around

a lady's slender throat.

Your abuela with her quick hands sewed lace of light silk

in teardrops, in sacred shapes, in secret languages

for the top of the lady's hair.

Mantilla.

For granny, tatted cotton in a time of Calvin,

in evenings of simmered longing.

For abuela, spun silk atop mother of pearl

in days of dark passages spoken threats hushed hopes.

My grandmother's platted dark hair, grey's lavender,

locks dancing in grandfather's face.

Your abuela's black braid reaching to her waist,

woven at dawn as pink sun peers into the courtyard.

Granny sets the collar just so, for church.

Abuela pins the mantilla into her hair for masa.

Balms, offerings.

Resignation.

I just see fury now. Petulance.

People seared in disgust.

Pulled hot steel to protest softness

of woven cotton to cover the nose, the mouth.

Against change against rules against the offerings of science.

Find your religion.

Mine's in the pattern of the silvery checkerspot.

Just cotton-mouth me, an offering.

Mama's Quilt

by Vincent J. Tomeo

Life stitched together in threads so thick to bind one to another
Each patch tells a story.

A little girl with pigtails and books,
Staring at apples on a stand, bread lines, and tattered clothes.

Grandma, "A stitch in time will save nine."
1942, " War Bride." One square for a wedding will do.

A young woman in a vocational high school making machine guns
Part of the Home Front, wearing her love for country,
Flag, weapons to win The War, ration books, and victory gardens.

War won.

Baby footprints and then three more.
Off to school in Buster Brown Shoes, and caps, and gowns.
A single parent.
Daddy didn't come home.

Mama, baking bran muffins and apple pie.
Escorting children off to school.
Praise the Lord! They are growing strong.

Quilt: Susan Leitzsch

Photo: Harry Morrow

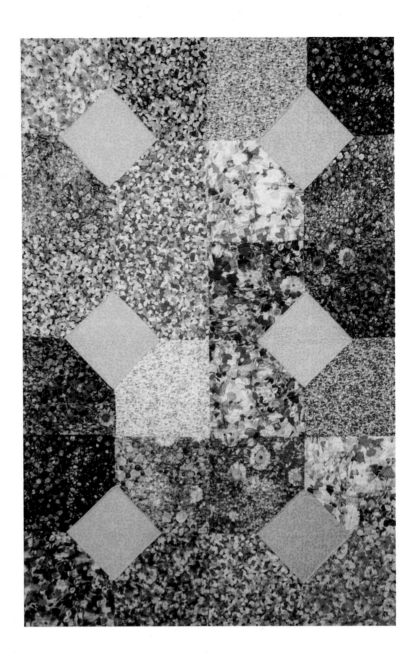

Life is a river flowing.

Time passing.

Squares, circles, triangles,

pentagons of earth break away to form another bed, another day.

See the flowers, birds, bees.

Children are grown.

Three children start anew.

Life is a blanket stitching, sharing, caring, loving, nurturing, kind.

So too, Like the Sun is to flowers.

A Comfort Blanket colored bright,

Spurs dreams of The Greatest Generation Quilt.

Quilted Family

by Linda Ankrah-Dove

The girl turns on her bedside lamp. The banging down below
bounces the bedroom floorboards and she is wide awake.
Only three o'clock. Hours yet till school.

She sits up chilled, draws blankets round her.
From the basket a thimble, scissors, box of pins,
mother's reel of thread.

The yelling, a clattering down of mountain rocks,
drains into murmurs, then pools into the silence
of a hollow nowhere.

She shakes out a rag, once his red plaid shirt.
She cuts it square, then a scrap from her old nightdress
striped black and blue.

She aligns the two, pieces them with pins, a temporary match
before the tacking. She continues cutting, pairing, pinning
reds with blacks and blues.

The back door bangs. The floor vibrates. She pricks her thumb,

sucks the bead of blood like a baby would for solace.
She piles her pinning work next to the sewing basket.
Nearly time for school.

Down In the kitchen, a torn blouse slung on mother's chair,
beer spilling from the table, a glass mug
shattered on the tiles.

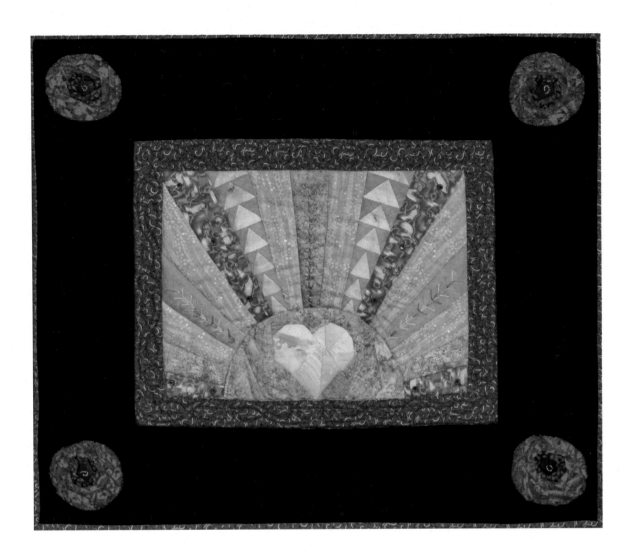

She grabs the blouse, rips it, hurls it on the floor,

scrapes it up with spattered splinters,

wrings it out.

Blood seeps from between her fingers and drips

like tears between cracks in the tiles, red tears

mixed with black and blue.

Prayer Quilt

by Mark Hudson

A bunch of women from my mother's church built

a healing gift for her cancer, a prayer quilt.

The quilt hung from the church for weeks,

people added threads so the spirit could speak.

People would tie a knot on the string,

and up above the angels would sing.

The cancer was healed, and God was praised,

and everybody who prayed was amazed.

From Florida, they sent the quilt to mother,

it was hung on her wall like a giant cover.

It showed that God's arms cover us all,

the quilt symbolized God's love on the wall.

But now in Florida while on vacation,

The cancer came back to all our frustration.

The quilt seemed like an answer to prayer,

but now I can show my mom that I care.

The cancer returning is bad news,

it's the reason I feel such blues.

My mom will have to take chemo once more,

so the quilt is something I do not adore.

I hope my mother receives God's will,

that she'll go to heaven if she's really ill.

But either way I'll be here on Earth,

it's hard to feel too much mirth.

If it's my mama's time to go,

I hope she knows I love her so.

(Dedicated to my mother, Lynne Hudson, who passed away from Ovarian Cancer)

Quilt: Berta Goldgaber   **Photo**: Harry Morrow.

Threads

by Sofia M. Starnes

Around the bend, across a field; aware

of hours, attuned to years: always the women

of those worlds return to us, bearing their

pieced afternoons as gifts. Hexagons again,

swaddles of untangled wear, these hidden

women venture out of their groves for us,

become texture through us. Without a fuss,

they lift the threads spooling around a fleet

of children. Ours now the recurring rus-

tle… Pinafores from waists, booties out of feet.

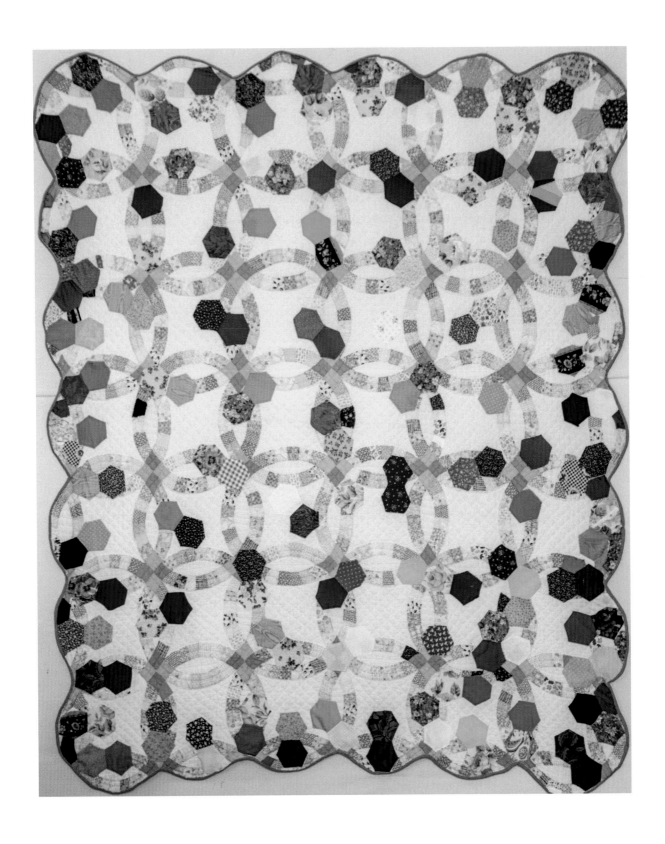

Quilt: Edna O. Starnes & Sofia M. Starnes   **Photo**: Harry Morrow

My Mother Sings of Love

by Luisa A. Igloria

In the common room, the nurses wave
their arms as if conducting a symphony—

Almost folded over in her chair, my mother
opens her mouth: pale-headed bird

with arms enclosed in soft volumes of
sweater sleeves. By what emerges,

it's clear she still remembers the lyrics
of a love song: whole segments with

refrains about promises, but also unfaithful
loves. She used to practice standing

by the piano, folding both hands close to
her chest so the slightest pressure

produced a marbled vibrato pulsing. She
has it, still— how to send that voice up

the ladder of the throat from out of some
deeper unknown, as though testing the exit

she'll surely take one day into the rarer air
surrounding this temporary home in the world.

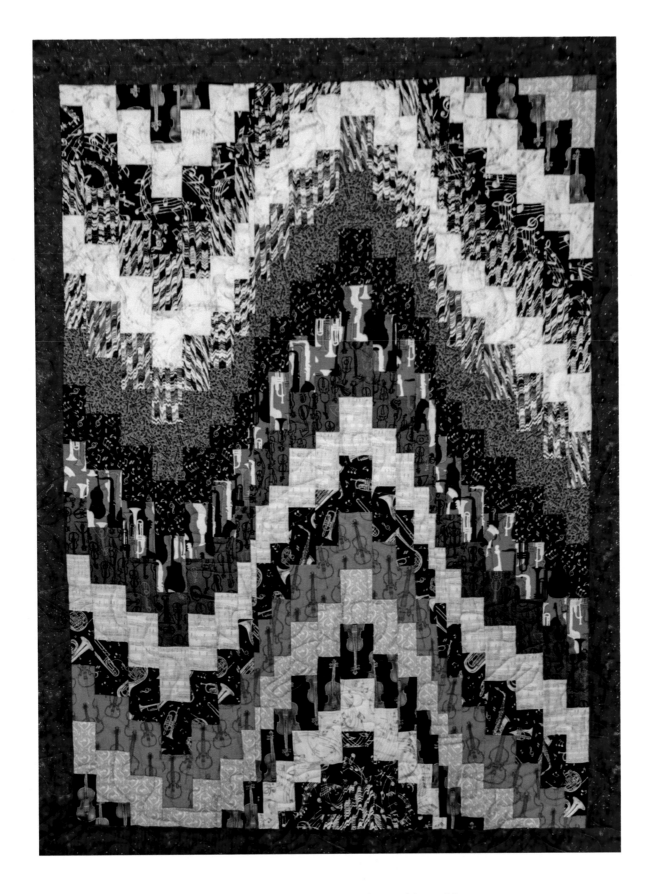

Quilt: Kathleen P. Decker   **Photo**: Harry Morrow

Violin #1

by Stacy Clair

Five a.m. and she calls my name

The air is calm and undisturbed

It's the perfect time to touch her

I am drawn to her

She is my addiction

Her body is smooth and curvy

A smile breaks my lips as I reach out

She quivers under my touch

I lift her to my face

I inhale her sweet, sweet scent

I ask her to sing for me

She remains silent

She's waiting for me to put my hands on her

Waiting for my fingers to touch her in the right spot

I do so and she trills a beautiful melody

It's just for me

She sings only for me

I know just what to do to pull the music from her body

Hours later and she still trembles as I run my fingertips down her neck

I can feel the mesmerized eyes of the audience as they share my private moment

I glide the bow back and forth, faster and faster

The feeling becomes more and more intense

I can feel the breath catch in their throats

I can see their eyes invading mine

I make her sing for them

As the final note is held my own breath catches

I feel her body begin to calm underneath of mine

Quilt: Ann Czompo   **Photo:** Harry Morrow

Five p.m. and she whispers my name

The air is full of static electricity

It's the perfect time to lay her down to rest

I pull her gently from my face

I thank her for the magical music we just made

I exhale and walk off the stage

Mother Alyce

By Ricci

Chose whorehouse pink to paint your walls

(though purple was your color);

Looks stately with white lace curtains and all your curios

gathered year after year from child/grandchild.

Baking bread fills the air, beside the coffee scent.

Spider plants turn green the light that softly filters in.

Two dozen odd stockings crowd the stone mantel piece.

Bake cookies with generations drawn together 'round you.

Quietly or loudly lead us in stories of old friends.

Sow lemon drops and warming hugs.

Quilt: Shirley Buchanan, quilted by Beth Filko   **Photo:** Beth Filko

My Aunt's Pie

by Karen Sparrow

My aunt stirs and whisks

Folds, sifts and whips

Everything measured exactly

Sugar, spices and extracts

Then baking, timing and cooling

It's so hard not to start eating

Her cakes and pies are better

Than the rest

But her lemon meringue

Is the best

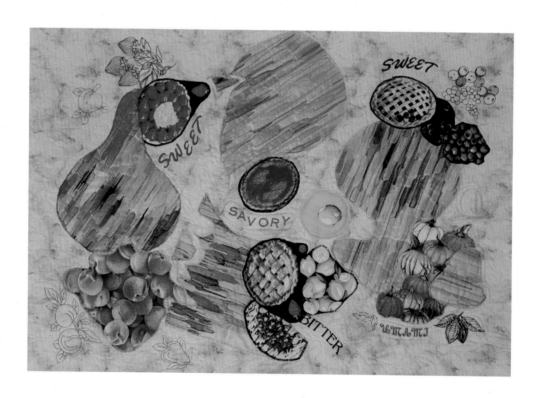

Quilt & Photo: Kathleen P. Decker

Quilt: Susan Moeslein

Photo: Harry Morrow

Baking Day

by Terry Cox-Joseph

I never expect the spoken word to be magic
yet when it flows from his lips
it is a miracle created like grandmother's
recipes. Roll, punch, knead.

Ten cups discipline, twenty extra-tight hugs,
a thousand denials, dollop of peanut butter,
three police encounters, one packet occupational
therapy, three hundred milligrams lithium.
Flour lightly. Bake on low for a lifetime.

Harmony, Carbon, Oxygen—listen! Murmurs.
His words, spoken words, sentences
fill the air with scent of yeast, warm bread
and insight, rising reason, stability.

Grandmother knew to open the oven
gently
so the cake wouldn't fall.
Tiptoe. Wait.

The Burden of Things

by Frederick Wilbur

My mother's house,

(a hoped-for mention in *The Magazine*

Antiques), is appropriately

appointed with artifacts—

Tiffany silver, Vermont tin ware,

hand tatted lace,

hand-painted porcelain and trays

of English *papier maché*

a local artist's line drawings,

and lots of less-than-perfect—

an inventory envied by those

invited in for instruction.

After her long passing,

her personal passions

became legal

and the last known Will left thoroughly documented

details of their dispersal.

She had snipped

and scrapbooked Sotheby's sales figures,

pride's own order which others

don't appreciate—

trustees, testy siblings,

and tired lawyers

who only wanted to warehouse

her worries.

And I, as trustee, caught in conscientious caring

would rather the ragged quilt

or rippled

grain of grandad's gaming table,

or Dad's temperament,

Taunton accent,

because memory

is what money

cannot buy or mend.

NATURE

Quilt: Catherine Swetnam, quilted by Amanda Lightfoot   **Photo**: Harry Morrow

Barred Owl

by Lawrence Bertram

I saw a huge Barred Owl today

With wings as wide as mine.

Framed on a leafless branch

Under a blue filled sky.

Reigning over frozen white

Including me and mine.

It passed on spending time on me

No call, no who, no rhyme.

His look straight, without judgment

Until he perceived my gaze.

Then he flew off right at once

Into the breaking day.

Had he been out there all the night?

Waiting just for me.

To tell me only recognition matters,

That the rest's just foolery.

Quilt: Michele Hoffman, quilted by Beth Filko   **Photo**: Harry Morrow

A Hawk and an Owl

by Mark B. Hamilton

Opposite Saint Genevieve,

I sit with a hawk and an owl

near an open pit mine.

The whistle signals the end of a work day,

but the docks keep loading lime, sand, and coal:

Crane buckets plummet like thunder,

conveyor belts grinding into a roar

under the arc of floodlights.

I camp across the river

beneath dark cottonwoods. And deeper back

there is a breaking of branches,

A buck scraping his antlers, and bawling out

his love song.

The fire crackles,

the north wind kicking up a little

excited starlight.

(First published in *Umbrella Factory Magazine*.)

Quilt: Debbie Noonan, quilted by Martha Berry   **Photo:** Harry Morrow

Mid-Winter Encounter

by Ed Lull

Loose driveway stones crackled under tires

as I approached my garage,

biting cold and dark as tar.

High beams illuminated the garage door

and newly trimmed vitex bush.

My vision fastened

on the bulky object on branch stubs,

at eye level and motionless.

It was an owl, wings folded,

unruffled by my presence

or by being on stage, in the spotlight,

surrounded by blackness.

Emerging from the car, I stood still,

exchanging stares with this regal creature.

A large head, flat face with glistening eyes

and short, hooked beak,

sat atop a hawk-sized body

with speckled brown feathers.

Although I have heard owls at night,

I had never seen one up close.

I stood a dozen feet away, like a statue,

my sense of awe growing.

Suddenly his head swivelled,

as if on a well-oiled bearing.

Nothing seen, he resumed his curious gaze.

What thoughts danced behind those blazing eyes?

What instincts assured him I was no threat?

Quilt: Catherine Swetnam, quilted by Amanda Llghtfoot

Photo: Harry Morrow

This marvelous bird remained placid,

until garage door creaking broke the spell,

disturbing the equilibrium of the encounter.

I experienced a strange sadness

when, with a whirr of waving wings,

he vanished into the night.

Backyard Philosophy

by Anne Roseman

"The sleep of reason produces monsters"
Goya

Late afternoon is a time I often sit
Outside to observe my bamboo forest
Knowing deep down the roots reach out
Connecting in a cross-stitched pattern
Like the quilt covering me.
A wind picks up and I wonder-was this in the
Weather forecast for today? I wonder, too, what
Is that sound from the bamboo forest? It is more
Than just the wind. Listen: "hoo-hoo'to-hoo-ooo."
Three times I hear this and then, flying from the
Bamboo forest, straight toward me in my chair are
Three owls. Yes, my family, my owl family, and I
Think that this is finally my time.

Murmuration of Starlings

by Sally Zakariya

Dancing in the eastern sky
a bird cloud pulses out,
draws in, widening
and turning all together—
a swirl of starlings,
wings in synchrony,
each bird imperceptibly,
invisibly, communing
with the birds nearby,
balancing uncertainty
and consensus.

A rule of seven, science
says, and more a matter
of physics than biology—
each small group poised
on the edge of transformation,
like crystals forming, liquids
turning into gas, metals
becoming magnetized.

But what a wonder, this
murmuration—a ribbon
of flight unfurled against
the sky, eddy and churn
of a thousand wings
thrumming with life.

Quilt: Corrine Vance   **Photo**: Harry Morrow

Last Night I Dreamed I was a Hummingbird

by Patrice D. Wilkerson

My eyes grew tired

From such a gruesome day

As I lay in my bed

My mind drifted away

I felt so free

Without a care

It was just me and the sky

What a dynamic pair

I could go anywhere

And do anything

I didn't have to worry

About a darn thing

No stress, no heartache

Or no pain

For once in my life

I felt relaxed and sane

Forward, backwards

And upside down

I'm having so much fun

Flying around

Quilt: Catherine Altice   **Photo**: Harry Morrow

I can sing I can dive

And I can soar

The life of a hummingbird

Is never a bore

As my alarm went off

I had to say goodbye

Oh, how I'm going to miss

The life in the sky

Secretary

by Diana Woodcock

One sighting of the Secretary bird

on the African savanna, I'm a goner.

Sagittarius serpentarius, regal –

a cross between a crane and an eagle,

with its fierce demeanor, a raptor

with a hooked beak, apt for attacking

its prey. Long legs fitting for the runway.

Breathing in, breathing out, I am one

with him. Other birds moving about –

Laughing dove, Levaillant's

cuckoo – they all call and coo,

but all I can do is focus on the Secretary.

A cool dull February morning,

a fine mist of rain falling, my only

task all day to watch birds and connect

passion with words.

Thanks be to this African flood plain,

season of rain, birds cruising through grasses.

Global warming alarming for everything

whose rituals are tied to this lion-colored

land. The rains came late this year.

But now the teaks are blushing pink,

thorn trees flaming, marula dropping

its hard green fruit – not yet ripe enough

to entice the baboon troupe.

Quilt Carla Esposito **Photo**: Harry Morrow

I linger with one elegant Secretary
on the threshold of spring, everything
holding its breath, like a caesura
in which the universe keeps still
for one instant – the bird concealed
in shadows of leaves and branches,
revealed by a breeze or slightest turn
of head.

I watch stalled enthralled
by the life of this one long-eyelashed
raptor I shall be singing the praises of
forever after.

Quilt: Taylor Potts   **Photo**: Harry Morrow

48

Amorphous

by Laura J. Bobrow

Atop the blades of grass in morning light,

Many are the drops of sparkling dew.

Out beyond the barn two doves take flight

Rendering their somber calls, *tu-coo*!

Presently the cows begin to stir.

Honeybees begin their pollen run.

Old tabby cat awakes and licks his fur

Underneath the warming of the sun.

Softly now his day has just begun.

There Are So Many Wonders In A Cow's Head*

by Catherine Malley

Cow tongues curl around

the yellow grass, soft mouths

tug withered shoots. Enormous brown

eyes gaze beyond easels and bobbing heads.

The sun moves just above the oxblood

barn; rays bounce off the silver silo, cast

tonal shadows. A ribbon of distant hills undulates;

light smolders oaks gold, maples, scarlet sugar.

Colors shift under cloud wisps.

What do cows think of artists in a

farmer's field as they conduct silent

paintbrush symphonies, layer impasto

tiers of thick color? Brushstrokes

of buttery light, blue shadows, milked clouds.

ÞAÐ ERU MARGAR UNDUR Í HÖFUÐKÚPU" (An old Icelandic saying)

Quilt: Penny Haag   **Photo**: Harry Morrow

For My Hands, for My Village of Eyes

by Erin Newton Wells

As the silken churro sheep move in one smooth cloud
over wheatgrass and silver sage, so with my hands.

They reach into this dream, how it began with scent
of rain and shadow, its cloud pulled into my hands.

Take it and see the light rise, the world made again
and telling its long story on the palms of our hands.

The land sings itself alive, sings up gray mountain,
its juniper and piñon through fingers of these hands.

Roll it and shape it, let it become one long dream
of saltbush where sheep may rest within our hands.

Give them small pools for their thirst, pools like eyes
where passing cloud drifts above these many hands.

Name us for the water, let it curl like horns of sheep
as it tumbles into streams from my hands, our hands.

Let the world remember long grass made into song,
and song into marigold and yarrow for these hands.

The world whispers soft wool. Gather it to pass
from my hands into your hands, and to your hands.

Writer's Eye Prize, 2019, based on Hand Spinning,
Village of Los Ojos, NM, by Maria Varela.

Text within image: DAMARALAND · village of Fonteins Pos · goatherders · farmers · Anna · the laundress

Quilt Jody Gruendel   **Photo**: Harry Morrow

Menagerie in the Pandemic

by Susan Notar

With people in isolation, wildlife itching to roam reclaim land worldwide.
W. Post, April 16, 2020

Mountain goats in Wales
now roam the empty streets
stick their curly-horned heads into flowerboxes
trip along cobblestones in front of pubs
party in parking lots.

Dolphins arc in clear canals in Venice
in waters no vaporetti, or speed boats cross.

Baby sea turtles toddle into the waves
along Brazil's northeast coast
undisturbed by curious tourists
uneaten by hungry dogs.

Wild boars busk outside Gaudi buildings in Barcelona.
Peacocks preen in city parks.
Mountain lions nap in trees near restaurants in Boulder.

This unexpected benefit of our social isolation
reclaiming what is theirs
telling us where to go.

Previously published in *Artemis Journal*, June 2021.

Quilt: Kaye McWhirter   **Photo:** Harry Morrow

River Made of Dragon

by Erin Newton Wells

–after Chen Rong, The Nine Dragons, 13th century handscroll

Nine of them, number for sky
in the Book of Changes, the sky a space
you might think of their bright wings unfurled,
if they had wings, nine,
highest single number, therefore exalted,
as dragons should be. But these
want water as their element, more crocodile
than avian, more serpentine in flow,
many scales, one hundred seventeen—
nine times four for yin, nine times nine
for yang—their claws each with five talons,
therefore noble.

Some say dinosaur bones inspired them,
a dragon image found in a grave seven
thousand years old. But in its black depths
the river has always carried
their churning to the sea, taking land as treasure,
bringing silt as gift, transmuting scales to rain
so crops grow, so ocean basins fill, and fish
flourish in flickering silver.
Sit here and see how water becomes these nine
coiling things. Or nine times nine times nine.
One carries the flaming orb of sun, or the moon,
or a pearl.

It gleans from below or catches the reflection,
holds it to us in the promise
of good fortune. You must take it,
when offered.

Previously published in *Valley Voices*, 2018..

Quilt & Photo: Christie Eckardt, quilted by Classic Quilts Dubai

A Tortoise

by Derek Kannemeyer

Sunshine at last, & the woodland walks dappled with it.

On a patch-speckled side-path skirting a pond,

an immense tortoise, sunning itself.

Sshh, she said, as if they had been talking too loudly, or at all,

& tugged him back behind her to the trail.

Until it in its turn wound by the pond,

sludge-green, thick with algae & bottles, & where a tree trailed

bent-trunked over the bank they leaned to peer across it.

There, that mud-bronze mound: the tortoise. Would it crawl

off in the grass? Amend its angle to the sun? Trouble itself

to catch them looking? But it made no move at all.

And really, if it were to, would whatever it might do

reward the wait? They paused, unsure. But to outwait it,

an ancient tortoise on its sun-mullioned trail,

was beyond their capacities. He plucked trash from the pond,

a plastic bag's worth; she snapped some photos;

they moved on, prattling. Oh, the size of the thing, like a football!

How green the woods were, in the sun, after the rain!

The petaling, companionable byways; this brisk slow lane nowhere at all.

Quilt: Priscilla Stultz **Photo**: Harry Morrow

Memories Wander These Woods

by Amanda Sue Creasey

Thud of boots on roots

Wind in trees, rushing water

harnesses jingle.

Stars fell, burst to blooms

shining in the grass, twinkling

in the blades of green.

Realize green is

really a million different

colors. Ferns unfurl.

Stump, stark and stately,

refusing indignity

of death, solid still.

Jack-in-the-Pulpits

White sock waiting on the trail

Reflection, rebirth.

Whispers of memories

wander always through these woods.

You, still by my side.

Quilt Susan Voigt   **Photo**: Harry Morrow

Birches

by Kathleen P. Decker

swaying birches

for the most part

unbroken

white bark greyed

by fog

peeling, peeled

battered by high winds

and hail

forest turned ominous

and then

the blessed sun

beaming

their bark shines

with golden hues

that reflect the light

into the floor below

animals peek out

from storm hides

forest turned bright

Quilt & Photo: Kathleen P. Decker

A Fivefold Path

by James Irving Mann

Prepare

in

Wisdom

Plant

in

Faith

Harvest

in

Love

Share

in

Joy

Live

in

Peace

Quilt: Beth Filko   **Photo**: Harry Morrow

Frosty Forest Soldiers

by Pamela Brothers Denyes

I watched with quiet joy today

as the dawning winter sun danced,

glinting through frosty forest soldiers

rising silent and tall above the earth.

Shimmering sunrise rays, slanted in January's

reclining posture, shone briefly on each tree,

as though shining through a chilly thirty-foot

high slit In the day's busy schedule.

Warming light revealed the beech's speckles,

the old pine's woodpecker holes, shiny

still-green ivy rising from the dark thick

layer of autumn-tossed leaves.

Then, quick as the fox disappearing at dawn,

the fickle beam moved on and away,

as if to awaken from their winter sleep

another sleepy squadron of forest soldiers.

Mata Atlantica

by Christian Pascale

Within my mind's rich canopy

I see the jungle green up high

Where golden parakeets can fly

Above the rocks and deep blue sea.

Blue-yellow parrots sing off key.

And screech, "Be on your way," to me.

Toucano, jewel-eyed, in tree,

Banana bill up turned in glee,

Knows the tropics belong to him.

The cliffs above the peaceful sea

Dare me to glide to sand, and swim

In soothing waters, wild and free.

Within this jungle of my mind

I see reflected for all time

The rainbow-colored tropic sky

That I would dare to versify.

Tidal Basin Stars

by Jacqueline Jules

Blooming first in bigger numbers,
the Yoshino get all the attention.
We hold festivals and parades.
People visit in throngs.

Two weeks later,
when the Kwanzan boast
fifty petaled blooms,
there's no TV coverage.

Apparently, a delicate five,
easily blown away
are more impressive
than sturdy pink clusters,
unbending in the breeze.

At the Tidal Basin and in life,
the cameras seem to love
what's first and most fragile
far more than those
who bloom the longest.

Quilt: Susan Novack **Photo**: Harry Morrow

Fallen petals

by Serena Fusek

Kimono sleeve--
from it she shakes
cherry blossom petals.

As they walked around the pond
petals fell.

After he leaves
taking her song
white petals
like falling stars
escape from her sleeve.

Her kimono
pink and white blossoms
printed on silk.
Petals fall from its sleeve.

He departs.
She shakes both sleeves
gathers the petals
one by one--

smiles at her own foolishness
lets them float from the window.

Some settle on the pond.

Next time she pulls the silk
over her body
two dried petals
will drift to the mat.

Spring's Desire

by Gail Newman

First thing, early morning,

I go out in my terry cloth robe,

just for a minute to take a look,

watching for whatever

companion has come up

in the night to welcome me.

What's new? I ask

the Drama Queens,

poppies with impossible

feathered petals looming

open in the sunlight.

Girls, I say, as they lean

chest-high into me.

The garden is cunning,

with lures of color, scent,

and crusted shadow.

I blow onto the flowers

the warm mist of my breath

as if I am just some light

breeze or brush of wing,

a presence, alive

in the sprawling world,

brimming with hope.

Petals

by Elizabeth Spencer Spragins

Quilt: Ann Czompo.

Photo: Harry Morrow

April wind waltzes

in the flowered arms of trees—

a brook hums softly

while she braids her silver hair

with fallen cherry blossoms

Previously published in *Waltzing With Water: Tempos in Verse*, (Shanti Arts Publishing, 2021).

Calla Lily

by Joan Ellen Casey

Stems stand clustered together
frocked in sheaths
of the smoothest emerald corduroy.

Leaves grown and unfurled
show thin lines of lime
that captured spring's sun.

Some reach to
ripple and bend, dip and point their tips
like acrobats.

Only the tallest
are burnished with fuchsia
from which springs a melody of pink and purple.

A symphony ensues
each player holding swollen hearts of pollen
that lay hidden and camera shy.

Zooming in creates a blur
of the beginning of color and the end of shape
and a background that fades away.

Being close tells no more
of liquid that glistens
at tapered ends of tips

pointing
like fingers between the creator and the created
or falling tears.

Iris of Spring

by Mike Maggio

Iris of Spring

you sprout luxurious

from your false bed of snow.

Enrobed in your splendid yellow and green,

so soft, so languid,

your willowy arms

outstretched,

your legs, concealed in a curious tangle

Your face, a wisp of woken wonder.

You unfold

quietly, tenderly,

tall and tempting

invite me to gaze, to touch

to linger

in your faint drowsy fragrance.

How came you to be like this?

What did you all winter

lying nestled in your frigid muddle of soil:

the earth, your covetous lover

the sun, feverish with want

the frost, a wicked reminder of your cruel absence.

Iris, I spy you couched in mystery

and yearn to seize you

long to capture your wondrous bloom

snatch you from your bold innocence
place you in a vase to adorn love's altar
to watch and wonder and adore.

Come now, let us not regret the future.
Let us revel in this brief moment.
Let us embrace this elusive season of bliss.

For Spring shall shed it silken sheen
Summer will rise,
then tumble into Fall

and I left here, alone,
as you surrender once again
to Winter's icy grip.

I shall await your resurrection.
Steadfast, I shall remain here,
agonized, canonized

as my longing, like the weeping stars,
endures the cold, bitter night.

Quilt: Susan Neidlinger
Photo: Harry Morrow

Water Lillies

by Emory Jones

In this mode, Monet was the master—

His *Bridge over a Pond of Water Lilies*

Is a perfect piece of suffused light.

Background foliage drooping, weeping,

Dipping leaf tips in the warm water

Centered on a graceful arch of bridge;

Blue-green water shimmering

With gold flecks

Splashed with black-green pads

And delicate white flowers—

We feel the warm sun,

The caress of gentle breeze.

Thank you, Claude.

Quilt: Stacy Bergert   **Photo**: Harry Morrow

Amen Roses

by Sandy Robinette

I bought a house

with a rose bush.

Not single, prissy buds

but day after day,

bouquet of scent and sight,

blushing richly

over a golden heart.

On the other hand,

in gathering such bounty,

I am scratched,

time and again

by sharp, relentless thorns.

But beauty calls for

abandon,

not caution.

So I'll add my red

life drippings,

as I collect my unexpected treasure,

a glory

of sunset roses.

Quilt: Jeanne Sanders   **Photo:** Harry Morrow

Summer's Splendid Shroud

by Rebecca K. Leet

The crepe myrtle's last

raspberry blossoms

kiss their branches goodbye

and feather the grave

of summer

Quilt: Hope Brans, quilted by Beth Filko   **Photo:** Harry Morrow

Blue Wild Indigo

by Yvonne Zipter

I have long admired their dark oval bodies,

wagging like chow tongues in the breeze.

Yet for all the pods' deep bruise of color

it's the plant's modest, green elliptical leaves,

with their secret concentrations of indican

(tryptophan's less sleepy cousin),

that yield the dye prized, once, by shamans,

slavers, rag traders, and kings, the powder

that was more powerful than the gun,

that was worth, in a length of cloth,

a human body. It's the pod's interior, though,

that's the real marvel to me, seeds lined up

like piglets at suckle, like rowers in a scull,

like socks in a gentleman's drawer, like

footlights glowing golden against the pod's

black backdrop, ready to illuminate the next

stage of their cycle: heroes of their own story.

The two halves of a pod rest side by side on my desk

like pages of an open book about some captives,

making their escape in two rough-hewn boats.

First published in *Heron Tree*, August 2019; reprinted in *Kissing the Long Face of the Greyhound*, Terrapin Books, 2020.

Note: Italicized line quoted from Catherine E. McKinley, from *Indigo: In Search of the Color That Seduced the World.*

The Get-Well Card

by Anne Metcalf

I pick the card

A childish sailboat

Bobbing against

A deep blue sea

Whitecaps etched

Across the foreground

With little inverted v's

Above in the clear bright sky

A sunny-side up

Lemon drop sun

With the same

Little inverted v's

This time extending

Glorious yellow rays out

Into the verdant

Hills beyond

Little farms and houses

And even littler people

Dot the faraway fields

Thus ends my summer

A simple card

Sent to a good friend

After a long stare

At a minuscule sailboat

Bobbing carefree in the sea

Quilt: Bonnie Timm

Photo: Harry Morrow

The Distant Lighthouse

by R. J. Keeler

Waves crash, crash effortlessly but recklessly.
She, the lamp keeper, also the weaver,
wanting to make woof the daughter of warp.
But warp commanded her, as did the wave

of deep and violent sea, meaningful but directed;
her weirs wove an overgrown ocean into tides.
Met and spray of wild seized against edged bricks;
lampreys sought crevasses along dark rocks.

She, both thinker and feeler; she, moth to light.
Her duties—to light the topmost lamp at dusk, snuff
it out at dawn, except if day be dark with storm,
then to rush shadows back to corners of the sky.

When she raised her shuttle—unbidden acrobat—
she transformed to servant, became accomplice;
a brave woman slowly wise, a sailship coming up
the channel, the whole of known time, a windspray.

The weaver talked and heard mainly with her hands,
then the high-promised light waited for her touch,
the wave of her palms. Now the waves the color
of lead; only at that precipice is there ever change.

On every other year, she forgets the sea's colors
woven into the deftness of her corse, her habit.

The Boat

by Eric Forsbergh

A small boat works its way, a couple aboard, young,

under a florid lake sunset. Even from a distance

they seem new to each other, their faces within a breath's reach,

their shoulders forward deferentially.

Her slim arms are by her side.

It's the eyes that carry all communication now.

Being in the confines of this boat, looks that fall away

must return to redirect the mouth's intent.

The motor burbles onward,

making slight headway under a vast sky.

With the sun behind, they are a mere outline

on an unsteady plane of mercury.

What is there in the flight of a single day?

There are no cogent messages

in the reddened half-illumination of their faces.

It is moisture and the play of light

in this blue that overlays the salmon,

peach, mango, running into streaks of pulp

from a blood orange seeming close at hand.

The last red lip of light hugs the fur-like hills,

all in utter silence. Leaning closer in the darkening boat,

hope picks its way among the words,

shifting weight from foot to foot, not knowing which to ask:

"Are you to be my brilliant vapor of a dream?"

Or "Will this moment fade to black?"

Quilt: Millie Johnson
Photo: Harry Morrow

A Gwynn Island Blessing for a Fair Sail

by Carol Parris Krauss

A long weekend in a cracked cottage leaning

on the Middle Peninsula edge. We pushed

kayaks to the Bay. Slipped the clove hitch

shore, coasted beyond the grasp and hue

of the blue crab. A scrub and oyster shell

shore at our backs. Knotty pines to knobby spines.

Bound by the Rappahannock and Piankatank Rivers,

this neck is hailed as the Boating Capital of the Chesapeake Bay.

I don't know about that or know the flow and cast of these waters.

I do know as our neon colored envelopes

slipped the cleats of Deltaville dirt, bobbled and balanced

gentle waves and drifted

toward the horizon, I didn't hear or see large yachts.

No rhythmic engine

purr. No tourist laughter cresting in my direction as they

sunned on deck. I simply spied the tip fin of the Sandbar shark,

accepted a Gwynn's Island blessing for a fair sail.

Clear Vision of Fading Sight

by Rebcca K. Leet

Remember the days

we stood in the crow's nest

of our ships

aft wind full

fair skies aloft

our bows sliced

blue-black sea

white clouds

stippled the sky

our world bore clear

demarcations

Now we rest main-deck

in the shallows

sails waft wearily

dusky clouds idle overhead

The sun sits lower on our horizon

but it paints the water

vibrant yellow and orange and red

and all the subtle shades

that swim between

a palette swirling

with life's passionate

equivocations

seen most clearly

when eyes have dimmed

and final furl

draws near

Quilt: Anne Trudel   **Photo**: Harry Morrow

Dear River

by Ellie White

I have always been good
at holding my breath, cycling the same
gasp of air from lungs, to mouth, to lungs…

Dear Wall, your safety seems dubious at best.
I don't doubt the quality of your concrete,
the soundness of your structure, or the hands
of those who wrestled you into being.
I suspect the hearts involved were ordinary, at worst.
I confess, I don't usually think in three dimensions
or recognize the sad lack of symmetry in sidewalk slabs.
My mistrust rests on a far less solid foundation
than your bricks. It is a voice, gentle as the waves lapping
at your side. It bids me to come closer,
to lean my back against your cool strength.

Dear River, I'm not sure if this salt on my skin
is yours or if it's just sweat. I'm not sure
if the salt of my body is the same as the salt
in the sea. I don't know where salt
comes from. I only know it lives
in my blood, which I sometimes crave
to feel on my skin like sweat.

Quilt:: Kathleen P. Decker, quilted by Beth Filko   **Photo:** Harry Morrow

Dear Wall, despite your continued willingness

to support my spine, I feel

that obnoxious sleeping-on-an-airplane wobble

starting to warp my neck into a swinging

handle. My head, as it snaps back, feels

more mallet than flesh and bone. When

you and I meet with an exquisite thud, my brain

suddenly feels more rubber than steel. This betrayal,

and the blood that never comes of it, make me

think Dear Hope is a transient bricklayer,

a builder of walls that must be maintained by those

who need them. And so I hold this salty blood in my body:

a deserted wall restraining a swollen river: a set of lungs recycling air.

Walk with Me

by Katharyn Howd Machan

Walk with me.

Walk with me to the river.

Walk with me to the river of fish.

The fish are small and fast.

The fish have no names.

The fish may call your name.

You may smile. You may answer.

Walk with me to where you may answer.

The river waits for us.

The fish wait for you.

They are fast and small.

In the river they are rainbows.

They will call the colors of your name.

Quilt: Mary Crandall & Julia Lewis, quilted by Jennifer Evans   **Photo**: Harry Morrow

Footprints

by Paul Evans Savas

Footprints in the sand,

Scattered on the shore,

With no path to follow,

Are the footprints yours?

Seek the Light of New Point Comfort,

Turn driftwood into oars,

Tides will wash away the imprints,

Golden sands await the morn.

SPIRITUALITY

Flowers, Fairies, and Me

By Sharon Canfield Dorsey

We used to converse, the flowers and I
on matters of import in days gone by.

The fairies appeared in bright mid-day sun
to giggle and dance and join in the fun.

Skylarks would entertain us with their song,
while quartets of bull frogs croak, croaked along.

I'd sit in soft grass beneath lacy trees
with ears tuned to music of buzzing bees.

Sometimes a bunny would creep up beside,
then quickly, nose twitching, run off to hide.

I didn't know then, the fairies would flee,
as time stole away the small child in me.

Sometimes I try to recapture those days
of magic and innocence 'neath sun's rays

through the eyes of the grandkids I adore,
as they talk to flowers outside my door.

Hamsa

by Fred Levy

Miriam, prophetess of the sea;

Fatima, Muhammed's daughter,

lend their names to this sheltering hand

in this land of endless war.

Fighters shatter the peace barrier;

no parting waters to help them survive.

Surviving but rarely alive,

she seeks my help

with hope disappearing.

Her eyes glaze, body shrinks

holding decades of pain.

Secrets bleed from a soul unmasked,

first a trickle then torrent -

nothing can conceal what the mirror reveals.

She faces the hamsa,

five fingers on her therapist's wall -

A hand…or fist?

Symbol of calm or man beating her down?

She scans for safe harbor,

her fear burns like napalm.

Within heartbeats

we wordlessly connect.

We breathe as one breath -

our eyes keep on speaking.

Quilt: Berta Goldgaber   **Photo**: Harry Morrow

Quilt: Shirley Buchanan, quilted by Beth Filko   **Photo**: Harry Morrow

Rothko's Chapel

by Sarah M. Sala

A spaceship to map grief's occipital orbit// A bloodstone door

If I had a choice, I would teach the politicians art

Or the words: sauce, poison, and praise

The self is a verb when the mundane fails solace If I had a choice: a comet-riddled night

A purple pheasant ascending

A double-hung window set ablaze

If I had a choice, a two-lane highway

A way out of the furnace

I Chase the Light

by Anna Buck

I chase the light, the detail

The color, the shadow

I keep a list of words, in my notes

For when I want

to artfully describe

The flicker, the glow

The flush in my cheek.

Mulberry, ash, olive, wine

Honey, marigold, indigo, clay,

Textile, tactile,

A thick, cool slab

A hot, dusty breeze

These words

roll around in my mouth

Bled, from my ballpoint pen

So my mind can rest

Quilt: Bonnie Smith, quilted by Martha Berry   **Photo**: Harry Morrow

When I Try for Color

by Curt Curtain

Get red on that canvas! Get red!

And yellow-orange—life!

Your colors are dead.

She's right you know.

My brush, though, it slithers into green

when red is what I mean to see.

Then, when I try a subtle slide

to pick up red the damned brush slips

on a spur of old dried paint

and comes up all amuck in gray;

or trying for a sly twist in pale gold,

it slides—I know I tried!—into blue.

But she's right.

A work of art needs life.

Nerves, it's nerves makes all the slip;

My critic's nerves are cool,

she never slips from red to blue.

She says it's all in the control. She says

my nerves spring loose and jar my aim.

It's true.

They splatter orange torment on my soul

I haven't the control for painting life.

Quilt: Susan Leitzsch   **Photo**: Harry Morrow

Joy

by Terra Leigh

You're a leaf

Easily swept away

When the wind plays

With my hair.

You're stepped on

With a sudden change in tone

Or forgotten manners.

You're crushed

By my overthinking,

Rejections from others,

Even being forced

To go through the drive thru.

But you're so heavy

That I know

The exact moment

You're gone,

And my entire day

Is a mess

Of routine notions.

It's a battle,

Keeping something

So fleeting,

But I'm ready.